With Love,

Alice Willitts

First Published in 2020
By Live Canon Poetry Ltd
www.livecanon.co.uk

© Alice Willitts 2020

978-1-909703-46-9

A CIP catalogue record for this book is available from the British Library.

Cover Photograph: Anna Watson

With Love,

Alice Willitts

Alice Willitts is a writer and plantswoman from the Fens. *Dear,* was published by *Magma Poetry* (2019) having won their inaugural pamphlet competition. She holds an MA in Creative Writing Poetry from UEA (2018). She co-edited *Magma 78: Collaborations* and runs the *#57 Poetry Collective.* She is a founding member of the biodiversity project *On The Verge Cambridge* and is collecting rebel stories on the climate emergency for *Channel Mag.*

For the one who is my light
& the three who are our shadows

Contents

it should be simple —
I want to write for you
the fabric of our lives
a garden for our years
seeded with the songs
of our children, I want
our passions I want the long
table of our conversations
the weakening hug of our
parents, I want to sew them
together loving each piece
as I pass them to you over
peelings in the kitchen
and trays of roast squash
or between our dirty
bikes and recycling bins
or out in the high dales
on that river stone
side by side, cheeks
bright, feet in flowing ice-
water, I want it all
every sweaty joy and hand-
made seam in the warm
garment of our love

LOVE 1

There is a form of mending known as Boro, which translates to rags, from the patched garments of the Aomori Prefecture in Northern Japan. The original garment is mended hundreds of times until the stitches themselves seem to replace the garment with decades of layering.

Boro stitches prioritise utility over embellishment. The stitches themselves are meant to patch the fabric while adding strength and warmth, not to serve as decoration.

The thought of a lifetime garment, where visible patterns of wear are celebrated, is a compelling metaphor for marriage.

you know this
inner ear voice
or the clatterattle
poppy seedhead
explaining
the longest love
to a wristy soil
as we pass by

I put my arms
fully around your cask
of gunpowder whiskey
to steady it tenderly
in the wheelbarrow
on the rutted path

To write the garment of our love. I touch it so tenderly. I turn it over in my hands. How stiff the fabric has become with age. I start by unpicking. I cut away the fraying, the way I trimmed our first baby's fringe. I tuck a sturdy patch underneath the hole like I used to fit sandwiches into his lunchboxes. I sew in bold, visible stitches to highlight the wear; honour each tug, each developmental milestone.

I keep the outermost lines to a running stitch; plain enough to secure the edges of the patch, bold enough so the mending stitches can shine. I mend not because our vintage love is broken but because it has been so well worn.

the clothes of a perturbed young woman
fast asleep, with a devil
sitting on her chest
are in a state of disarray

a boy cups sunshine in his father's hands
there are flowers

enter a black boar
with golden balls so prominent they splay
his hind legs as he trots
his young tusks are yellow

a hungry woman flows
from the tree of forgiveness
onto the blossoming back of her lover
he speaks: I am eating you
she speaks: I am eating you

Sometimes, the more we add the harder it becomes to see what was originally there. The more water and dust air contains the more immaterial the world seems. Mist-haze. Blur-haar. Dissolving edges. Rainbow-sunset. Harvest Moon. Pollution halo. Air is the medium of light.

The light in our garden is often green. I can say that. The sensual matters materially. Matter matters, the way my lungs breathe in wood and rock with each breath.

If our lives were millions long I would write about how the rock bends in the wind like a flower. How forests are brief as waves, drifting along the strange land, itself as constant as a butterfly.

why am I writing poems for you?
you have never read a poem to yourself
but it is the only way I know
to tell a thing

to know the person you are telling
makes telling it specifically
intimate
like I am given permission
to open the soil
and plant

I can believe a framework is a tried and tested set of rules for building.

Rules of this sort might be: darn the love you already own, mend to open the gap between buying and binning, refuse unethical loving, insist on an ecologically sound construction. Or are these slogans?

When the stone veneer of a library's facade slides off its glue; when the stuccoed breeze-block wall cascades in an earthquake; when the lime tree avenues die from disease; we feel tricked.

Women have not been expected to prevent breaking but to mend the damaged parts. Humming while they work.

do my jump-starts jolt you out of bed
into duty to the packed lunches
school bags and shaving?
because you leave me
every morning

When we are constrained by rules the result will be extraordinary. Caves are made by acid water using the rule of dissolution. If soft and hard rocks are ordered horizontally, acid water will experiment on the soft rock.

Hot water will dissolve frozen water. The result will be an extraordinary hole, the size of the Grand Canyon, under the ice in Greenland. Improvisations produce new patterns.

The deep context of a place matters. How many layers do we need to uncover to hear the language at work? How is a path made? Does it use a vocabulary of navigation? Never doubt that as few as fifteen committed passages over a site can create a distinct path, and more feet will follow.

How is a hole in the fabric made? We wear the same garment. We wear it out in different places.

with baffled amusement and deep love
you've watched me shul barefoot
and pinkly shivering
across grand costumes of sand
as the wild in me is sucked
into every icy sea

It might be said that if people think of this as an emergency, would models, would press, would buyers be flying around the world to see clothes? Would the world's natural resources be used for clothing women? Would they?

Dynamic fabrics answer to place and the needs of the specific beings that make their lives there.

Perhaps what attracts me to vintage love is the built-in nostalgia. A love with the added attractiveness of worn fibres alongside the durability of a work jacket.

I must tell you that poetry
is not a woman, as some poets say
I invite you to scan
any woman, the mollusc of her
where nature
gives up its formal presentation
of atoms for gloop

vain danger to open the saint of herself
frilled and gilling to the waters
whenever she is able
she closes against intruders
she finds it difficult
she keeps her jellied insides clean

you save the prettiest scraps of love
a shadow from the rusted
mattress spring that made
a heart or two carrots we grew
that wrapped around each other
a trespass sign we found saying
please keep close

LOVE 2

love

I want to join the strange community
of water snakes in not believing that
black-red parrots tell the tree where it ends
that nail-polish wrens are so dizzyingly small
the bush swallows fifty, that evening cranes who dance
neck to wingtip and weave the dusk, know us,
so young in the wonder of our world

love / how could I have known you'd be there?

no more alone — your floor, a meal, a heart
nestled in your buttered spaghetti and peanuts
with broccoli on the side or tucked up in your bicycle
chains, helmet and spanner fixes sheltered
by your council tax, mortgage and water rates
blessed by your photos (of sidings and hoardings)
framed and hung in this silly poem, a list of our love
that this silliest of poems lists, is a love of young persons
chasing each other around a cassette and half a pint
on the hot streets of Hammersmith where I've arrived
with my suitcase of unsurprising things
on the jaw-drop of your doorstep

love / paperclipped for life

I'm fine, happy,
fine, I say
paperclipping
myself into bed
at neat intervals
along the edge
of the duvet
duvet to pillow
me to sheet
sheet to mattress
tight, all paperclip
secured
I'm fine I say
you look unsure
you reach over
to trickle
a handful
of silver
paperclips
over my exposed
neck
to pool
in my hollows
tiny silver
paperclips
wholly
unsuited

to cloth-clipping
but I love
the gesture
I would
kiss you
maybe you
remember
sometimes
the diamond
engagement ring
we didn't buy
the one that
glistened
with the promise
of old age
but shone
a spectrum
of desire
so seductive
I feared
it would be
the ring
or you
I make
bracelets
from your
delicate
paperclip trickle
satisfied

love / couples who sleep in separate rooms live longer

this morning un-beds itself into a google result
        but I can't give you up
I live for your limbs piled near mine
        for hands that unwrap me
in sleepy meetings, how we
        drift off afterwards in our one damp skin —
remember, how we used to lie
        wrapped in each other every night
when there were no habit hollows
        when we slept any side of the bed
when bed was each other —
        so I can't give up your lumpy sleep
for a few more hours of daylight
        at the other end of life
when this morning I can open a dozy eye
        right into your precious face
feel my late body smile, shoo
        tangled wishes, you are all mine
to watch as you sleep, to love
        each wrinkle we've given and taken
because your face this close to mine
        makes me happier than anything else
and if you open your eyes and see me too —
        we'd lie here like two dopey adventurers
come to the treasure we had all along
        bathing in our own silly luck, to still be here

love / when you said start with Lucretius, I started with our firstborn

I couldn't remember the nature of thingness
because our new baby was noodling about in my head

because his new heart was tapping at mine
even as we sat in the cafe far from where he was.

I wonder if the heart-shaped leaves of the epimedium
you gift me will make enough shade for his future

and I picture me then, a young mother of right dreams
taking a moment in the dark garden

somewhere to breathe after a night feed, to be thankful
in a ripple of moth beats and the cool stretching of green.

It is only May. I do not sleep. I have not slept.
Keep the plant in this pot you'll say, plant it out in the autumn

under a tree or in a damp corner, it has yellow flowers like kisses
but my minds eye will go to his tiny hand unfurling as he sleeps

how it takes my heart again as I wait for that first full-body-jolt
the one where he will vault away and now I can move him

dangle him by his toes if I wish, nothing will wake him —
and there is your Lucretian moment, rough about the edges

made so simply from the dense matters of the day, but there.
Eight again, in a science class where with a single puff of smoke

Mr Jobling shows us how atoms jostle through the still air.
How, in that moment, the whole nature of things makes sense.

How to this day, I hold a vision of myself
less as a mother and more as a shape of atoms and voids —

atoms and voids that I cannot see
only there is a sense of self in a dark shape

in a dark garden in a dark night
a night where I hold myself in wonder at my beingness

at his beingness and how my heart will break me one day
when I have to leave him and suddenly my void will feel too real

and the dew will describe my skin as the first edge
of his world once more.

love / as only we can

your lever voice slips
a syncopated beat
and our limbs roll up
closetight like we tangoed it —
questions rattle our brilliant bed
you ask, do you think, should we,
perhaps lunge at each other now
like our parents did —
it matters how I say nothing

love / I think Seneca knew about the hares too

here, I'm tossing you the original need for love
and in its throwable lightness warn you that death will also come

you have no choice but to make yourself available for that my love
so why not catch my invitation and trot out today, hand-in-hand?

go where the hare flips and careens towards the field's edge
his slippery, black-tipped fear punching at nothing — that's us you know

and his leaping at air loses him nothing but dignity says the stoic
but now look at the cool taut hare sitting under the moon

attuned to every slap of animal in the radar of her ears
how she holds dread comfortably in her belly

how momentariness soaks her, lopes gently aside
as if she is no less than the field of all possibilities

love / under an apocalyptic pressure for a solution

can't
I just
come
fix
the shed
roof
with you
in the
hazy
blue
morning
and kneel
side by side
tap
tacks
through
the giving
tar
in the
satisfying
smell
of
a blackberry
dew

love / yesterday or sometime

I'm absorbed
making
something for you
when I drip
glue
onto the front pocket of our love
and it sticks
shut fibres
pulled into the knit
grip
but even as it dries
I say to the pocket
I'm sorry I'm sorry
last year sometime
you're absorbed
making
something for me
when you drip
glue
onto the back pocket of our love
and fibres
pulled by the grip
knit
how you
never say
sorry

love / at the we of our beginning

you are a rare animal, delicate
       as a glass sponge, your pointed stars overlap
in a complex structure of marvellousness
       that creates an internal current and expels so little
you who need nothing you don't make yourself, choose me
       and I am witness to the electronic synth
of your thoughts, that detangle the possibilities of code
       seemingly infinite in the minutes hours weeks years
of the precise exercise of care
       in bodied rooms with ceiling panels
and an open plan to make more artefacts
       in intricate, handmade programming
that speaks a lengthening language
       to vast data-sources in countries we will never visit
home to guzzling mega-computers
       the size of our country's GDP
invisibly making our world work

love / a wish

the brain simply can't answer parched seasons where colours
need water to survive. might tell the story
that one blue sky clouding doesn't steal another's crop

or that a dress sewn from velvet butterfly wings
doesn't pain us with bright spots of sunlight pressed open on
darkness. or ache for the loss of green green

but anybody who believes he's broken everything already
is capable of believing the fly loves its own burning —
let's open instead to the far moon

sing for the clouds to be pink
and exchange our bodies the way one stone
meets another stone and dissolves slowly through touching

love / life is change

after dark
you and I might
return to the fire
lay our foreheads
on dirt, cry —
you look at me
say quite plainly
that I light you
that you absorb me
here where red earth
was made blue water
was made yellow sun
warmed earth and earth
became a white star
and death was made
in its fabric
we can rise at dawn
can send voice out
like all voiced things
and show ourselves
to the light
as if we are already
our not-knowing children
we can dance feet
hard in the grass
chant with no words
stretch our arms
open as fen

reverent as the pulse
of a drummer
echoing a universe
potent in sun colours
with old sky rules
red, then blue
yellow, then white
and whoever said
the four ages of man —
we were wrong
we need to say
for the ages of
all living things
beating the song
in each cooling body
slowing its feet
to a swaying
in the rust damp
our silhouettes
are vanishing
along fossil lines

love / beats

the sharp tuning fork
of accelerant cells
sounds a clear C

we have caught a lump
in my throat, but what
is being operated on?
my singing
sounds empty
and it hurts like the surprise
of the bee sting
on my neck that day
when I was six

if we could sound that puncture
surely we'd whisper love
into each other, in time

love / and there love is

how I love you
even when you tell me and I know it's wrong
that our plane isn't on fire
[plunge]
that our planet isn't on fire
even when you tell me and I know it's wrong
I don't believe you are unterrified

and there love is
when you hold me so
I am kinder about seedlings
on every brink of giving it up
in this too hot greenhouse you are
the long drink of rainwater we needed
so my breathing slows and my muscles slide
a millimetre or two from their bones and I sag
into this moment in this rescue from the gripping
pain of nerves shot by the dark snake of lessons striking
by the wasp that will sting sting in agony by the bear roaring
at emerald salmon it cannot catch like all that I cannot do to save
the planet can be held so I am softer, and stronger, even when you let go

love / we can reframe the known savagery of loss

I'm not ready
as the day leaves my bag
with immense determination
we have delayed the night
as raucously as we can
while day packs up
its remarkable dark-sky trick
the way a child who isn't picked
for the team sags
                  your defiance
is relearning my hands
each black-splotched palm
feels darker than black
but as you cup and press
each one with a kiss
my pink fingers unfurl
hungry for light
                  my belovéd
this sickness has put
something like our trust in wonder
far away. Let's hold an open garden
for the rain —
tame my need to just hold you
in the can't-live afternoon
                  you'll go on
with your blue heart
out of my time
and I have seen a reflection

that mends our story
you will be released into tomorrow
weary and want-healing but weather-true
                              it's time, you say
to step outside thoughts
for a moment
onto the real grass
smell its cool green give —
doesn't that feel really good
under our feet?

love / we don't meddle with each other's flint

into the muddle of our hill walking
       an old wall has become a wind-spilled path
straight down the hillside where we wobble
       above bogs of heather and bilberry, shouting
no sane person would make a path this steep
       but here it is, raising the feet it once kept out —
marriage is made of walls that do not let you fall
       walls built of differences, bent to the shape
of their makers; firm walls that hold warmth, a place
       to lean and rest. Perhaps I peer round
your pile of stones with envy, marvel
       at the skill with which you pick and place any angle
eyeing my own wayward hands, instinctive or true
       we turn slip-ups into quirks and together we build
the enclosures and privacies of love —
       only now, in this year when you turn fifty
I understand that our tumbling walls
       will be paths for our children to pick their way
over a hill they have yet to climb; the hill, tinder
       to the wildfires of loving hard and holding solid
against the floods that come to us all —
       immediately and with gratitude
I know why I load our boys' pockets, anchor them
       to the land, stone by stone, their first wall
a kind wall that another walker will one day lean on
       will pick up a stone, will join them in the making

love / do you like green ants?

one time, a ranger would show us how
to pluck sharp green ants from trees

its legs would waggle
its body would arch

I would bring it to my mouth
suck its live abdomen off

a disbelief of lemon sherbet
would burst my saliva morals

I would do it over
taking like a child might

and again — I don't remember —
would you bite the green ants too?

love / if I were a mini-tutorial on love I'd say

fun should come to the party
hate should not be at the meeting
compassion should be hired
gratitude should be standing there when he gets off the plane
concern should see a specialist about the problem
forgiveness should be allowed to take part in the negotiations
duty should study harder for the final exam
betrayal should be waiting in another flat when we get home
tolerance should not take the job without renegotiating the salary
boredom should submit its research by the end of the month
passion should be admitted to the organisation
hope should take a gallon of water to get to the bottom of the gorge

love / I want you to know things

love is not morning coffee aroma! Love is singing to the hushed
audience knowing you are there to hear me

love is walking all the way to the cinema because I might bump
into you and we'll walk back dark-swaddled at elbow to hip

love is matching my sleepy breathing to yours, as if to invite myself in
when you're not awake

love is home-cooking and home-coming, laundry and
washing up, sowing and harvesting, knowing less as we get on

love is the diligent painful joy of feeling our way like academic
sculptors and risky potters in the only time that's ours

love does not smell of coffee

love / at fifty

I seek out your old pullover
slip on the ribbing of thick blue that is not teal
too much turquoise in it but not turquoise
which would need yellow or more green

but in its perfect dirt of blueness, I'm twenty again
padding about under the acrylic yarn of a sunday morning
naked and possibly smoking: the collar was lasciviously broad
it teased my thin shoulder as I sat on the back step

eyes closed while the sun made trees of my veins
and the new swallows skimmed the back-alley warmth
in those days you were lying in and I'd always be up before you
are you sleeping now?

I could, and I don't say should, I could wear this beloved sweater
naked today, sit on the back step with my garden of seeds at my feet
and let the sun make veins of me
let it wear away the stalking chill

why so frightened? of our plenty? what we've lost?
for our boys I'm frightened, how they'll die
too soon, how if they make it to fifty
the sun will boil their veins on the back step

or be the only antiseptic left
to think children might lie in rows with their mouths open
to the bright rays to kill strep throat
and this sweater, on loan for fevers, during labour and breastfeeding

on every lonely day after my mother died
or when we moved and again and again so tired
will we leave it for them, will they ever know naked warmth
will it smell of us?

love / same old sex my pretty elbow

my bones press too hard at joints and wear through fibres
till even my pretty elbow peeps out where it rubs at threads

snuggled like capillaries, snapping and fraying — a pretty elbow pokes
out of the muscle of our entangled lives the evening you stand behind me

close enough to breathe on my neck and see the pale, exposed bone
send a shiver down my arm — you tuck your finger into the hole

and stroke my pretty elbow to let it know you know — in the morning
I choose a patch — I've kept our old shirts and jeans, scraps

I cut a circle of shell brown and with pricks of pink, stitch down a pattern
like cats tongues, overlapping the loving that mends us

LOVE 3

This song I've been singing
About love
Its house is plain
Its clothes are darned
The ground
Is steady.
Outside
East of the sloping field
The brown river floods up
Where the poplars
Once spoke
A convincing
Language of air.
Flesh is
Microscopic organisms
I am a dwelt hulk
Of imagination
With unimaginable
Strength.
What is flesh
Scribbling
In plain sight?
The invisible largeness
Of our lives?
Is marriage
Actually
Made with the rules
Of stitching
And drystone walling?

Bone theory specifies
That bodies withdraw
From one another
Including the bodies
With which we measure them.
They are discrete.
A mark of discreteness is
The constant translation
[or mistranslation]
Of one body by another
Both wave-like
And particle-like
Flesh, brain, paper, repeat.
Is that how
The human sounds?
I, a kind of circling.
Love
A vulture feast *sagesse*
Shies away from.
Sing songs
Come closer.
No distasteful
Physical decay
Ever weakened
True love's pelt.

We had all the riches
In us
Under us
Around us
We were so hungry
So young, so cold
Sewing the scraps
Of what we had
Into something soft
To cushion our skins
From the light
From the ice
From death — sometimes
We need to stop stitching
Strip down and
Hold each other
Remember
What the heart beats for.
And in nature
It is written
We live only ten days
As adults.
In those ten days
He'll bring you such joy
You'll be delighted
To have had him
The way his silk body
Hangs like a devotion
Off his shoulders.

Use a total stranger
In such a way that they
Will not feel their time
Was wasted.
Thirst together
Open whiskey
Pour thumbfuls
Into the sun of your guts
Until the story
Cuts to the warm cuddle
And morning breath
Many years later
When sobering cancer
Lies in the throat
Of your Love.
Roll into my arms
Give your thumbs
To my ears
Block out
Our sobbing
Ease my body
From our bed
And hold me up
To the window
Until my goodbyes
Are the lines of silence
Trembling down the glass
And pretend
I'll come back as rain.

Let the live-lights
Of morning
Upend the dark
As the word
Slowly
Becomes Love's crutch
And stumble with me
Through each small save
Till we bump
Into the thing that faces us
The way eyes have always
Looked towards
Wonder.
Please.
Place my shaking hand
On its shoulder
Say *goodbye.*
Have we not been perfect
Bodies with our dew
Dreams? And, just like
Everybody else
We have to divine
How we love
Beyond
A grave we do not name
(describe the ways?)
Possible answer: yes
Possible answer: how

Use unique
Conventions
To make the sentimental
Fresh.
Try not asking
Permission
Try not asking but
Being.
Take words
And make them us.
Talk to other women
Ask how do I say this
In my mouth.
Always told
Without language
A thing cannot exist.
Quite perfectly
It can it turns out.
A poem is like seed
You say
Pushed into the topsoil
Of dead writing.
Write as if a tiger
Had sprung at you.
Write the stripes
The advertised gold stare
Do not flinch.
Put words into the gap
That protects you.

Of my love poems
I'm ashamed of using
My flimsy images
Of gardens
And underwater creatures
And ants. I mean
Who sucks ants
In love poems?
(a defence?)
He doesn't read
Poetry.
I wrote love poems
To an illiterate love.
If you can sew on flowers
That's one of your powers.
Together we find
Simplicity, honestly
Because love is complex.
Complex poems
Reassure me
Make me feel more at home.
Love's simple poems
Harrow me.
I want complex
Poems that reflect the inner life
Of that other, outer life.
You would not, could not
Read them Sam-I-Am

My love writing
Changes
Everything.
The mood of the old
Love poets —
Trying to become
Ignorant.
The clitoris is a bird
With balls.
Can I evolve into
What I haven't
Thought?
Love's Poetica
Lies open on the table
Whiskey clear in the glass
And Time doing what it does.
There was a time
When a man could read
All that was written
In his lifetime.
He was a poem   She memorised every line
He was a poem   But he can't read him
She is a poem   She likes to read over and over
Hang
The candyfloss of Love
On good bones

I love the love of love

Love
Is an odd word
To find in a poem.
My teacher said
If you can sew
In straight lines
That is one of your
Powers.
Sonnets (obviously) expect
Love and give it curtains.
Villanelles (less popular)
Make more silk while
The lines
Stitch themselves.
Song thrushes
Match the patterns
On snail-shells
They break.
The sestina (for poets)
Like every voice
Is real
Why would I bore Love
With mathematics?
Reality can turn out
Its own jelly moulds.
Silver cockchafers
Are pin tins
Stripping nights
Of their pinned seams.

Can the poet
Sound romantic
Trumpets now?
Shelley more or less said
A thousand
Sad-smiley-face stars
Stain a weak darkness
With their young tears
I say, pretty
Cosmic fire things
Veil our world's decay.
A world whose mighty wings
Were strong as blood
Extinguishes her kin.
A kin of the many-loved
Dark.
A kin whose music fears
To tread amid the pale
Dew-burnt breath
Of the animals.
Hearts bark
As they stalk away
Part rest-corpse, part feet
From a life always on the brink.
But let's be more specific.
In 2020, could we say
A mourner's first amorous leap
Is a thousand
Moonlight-birds?

Melancholy and sadness
Are prescribed as depression
And we are remembered as
Man-wept.
Our Adonais
Bare instead of burning.
Selfie with Earth's broken panting
His chest's vain shadow
His dull presence
In the perished wilderness.
Mountain panting
Saddest-splendour panting
Silenced fountain panting
Golden thunder
Gasp!
In a faded move
Sweet thunder tries her tongue
No moan-shadow
No gleam-heard
Fierce-flash
Hoary-glow
Nor vapour-usher no
Transfused-void
Nor shar'd-taper.
To tell of thunder now
We'd say, her vulval softness
Has great power.

Even as her flowers
Delight in Death
In grief
Thunder seeds are roused
That with a passion-winged nurseling
May yet outsoar
Man's monstrous spring.
It's truer now
Than ever.
Language that makes
Loves also makes
Lives.
We're told
Love lies
To the eye
Likes to mend lust
With the mind.
But I'm gathering
Materials.
Some things.
Some bits of worn out
Words with which to improvise
Fables, animated
For the moment
You are here
To caress
You.

Words
Buck at being
Closed in the page.
Maybe they are found again
Some out of use words
Recycled as sound.
Frozen water takes on
The colour of air
And if you believe taoists
The material essence of ice
Is the strength
Of its weakness.
A drystone wall
Is a shallow sermon
That I have
Summoned.
Poets are the poorest liars
That's one of
Our mending powers.
With Love,

Appendix

Love, how it hopes. Is so irresistible. I try hard to be serious but there is a tiny blond spider on my book. Two legs, dainty as hairs ticketing the top of the page asking if this is where she meant to be. She is very personal, local in the end, shimmering over the top and onto the page as if she can hear the same music as me. She is a living poem with body as noun leg as verb page as object hesitation as grammar. I translate her into the making of sound. I have no idea if she hears. Her eyes though. If I were spider it would be like shaving off all curls, putting eyes there, cutting off nose, ears, putting eyes there dragging mouth under chin, putting eyes there my once-face all eyes. Then. Then what she sees. Smooth paper fibre is a ploughed field in frost, clodden lumps of frozen earth I stumble over. She made it look so easy. To exist is to be possessed. I'd like to think she has laughter in her, in the micro-barrel of her top body. I want that as she rounds the page she might crease all her peculiar eyes and giggle a little to herself at a difficult field well crossed. We invented language when we could have invented eight legs skating here like mercury. How funny.

References

LOVE 1

I sew, and Katrina Rodabaugh introduced me to Boro in her book *Mending Matters: Stitch, Patch, and Repair Your Favorite Denim & More* (Abrams, 2018). Somewhat altered and patched, segments of Katrina's practical text feature in Love 1.

I also design gardens, and *The Language of Landscape* (Yale University Press, 1998) by Anne Whiston Spirn has been an important tool in my work and homage is paid to her landscaping language in Love 1.

LOVE 2

2019 felt hopeful with the first glimpses that environmentalism was turning the tide in favour of action. Lucretius' compelling physics in the *On the Nature of the Universe,* translated with such skill by Ronald Melville, captivated my thinking as I was re-reading it alongside James Lovelock's *Gaia,* so there are many references to their work threaded through the poems.

The subjunctive form is the language of wishes and longing. Love / if I were a mini-tutorial… uses exercises from https://www.englishpage.com/minitutorials/subjunctive.html

LOVE 3

'I love the love of love' is from James Berry's poem 'In Love', which moved me when I heard Raymond Antrobus read it to Anthony Anaxagorou during one of their InstaLive conversations in 2020.

I dialogue and quarrel with Percy Bysshe Shelley about his 'Adonais', although the highlighted section below (emphasis mine) could easily serve as an epigraph for *With Love,*.

> LIV
> That Light whose smile kindles the Universe,
> That Beauty in which all things work and move,
> That Benediction which the eclipsing Curse
> Of birth can quench not, that sustaining **Love**

Which through the web of being blindly wove
By man and beast and earth and air and sea,
Burns bright or dim, as each are mirrors of
The fire for which all thirst; now beams on me,
Consuming the last clouds of cold mortality.

Notes

'*Appendix*' started life as part of an ongoing, longform collaboration with poet
Laura Scott.

Grateful acknowledgement is made to the editors of the publications in which
poems from this book first appeared: 'love / when you said start with Lucretius, I
started with our firstborn', 'love / a wish', *Poetry Birmingham Literary Journal 4;*
'love / we can reframe the known savagery of loss', *Finished Creatures 3;* 'love /
same old sex my pretty elbow', *I'll Show You Mine Journal.*

I'd like to credit Juana Adcock for her exciting use of footnotes in *Split* (Blue
Diode), Bhanu Kapil for teaching me how to use the capital letter in *How To
Wash a Heart* (Liverpool University Press), and Aaron Kunin for *Love Three* (Wave
Books) that introduced me to Herbert's 'Love' and three-thinking. These poets are
the teachers who gird *With Love,.*

My personal gratitude to Helen Eastman and Glyn Maxwell for selecting the
collection and Rachel Goodman for your encouragement and hospitality.